Blessings, friend!

This focused **Bible Study for Women: Made Amazingly Simple** is designed to provide you with practical resources to explore God's Word, deepen your prayer life, and record your time studying the Bible.

It comes in two parts, which the *first part* guides you on **Reading, Applying, and Praying God's Word**. The *second part*, which is a study of the *Women of the Bible*, is designed not only to give you a direction and a framework, but to walk you and God on unpacking the scriptures together.

Whatever season you find yourself in, may this study encourage your spirit to delight in being a woman, uniquely and wonderfully made in the image of God.

Contents
Part I

PART I : INTRODUCTION
(Read. Apply. Pray.) /1

How to Use Section 1 /2

How to Use Section 2 /6

How to Use Section 3 /10

READ GOD'S WORD
Bible Reading Plan /13

The Life of Jesus /14

Exploring the Character of God /15

Bible Heroes /16

Foundations of Faith /27

Old Testament /31

New Testament /34

APPLY GOD'S WORD
Bible Study Templates and Acivities /37

- Book of the Bible Study /38
- Character Study /40
- Grace Bible Study Method /42
- Read Bible Srudy Method /44
- Topical Study /46
- Write the Word /48
- Verse Mapping /49
- 25 Questions to Help You Study God's Word with Confidence /50
- My Anchor Verses /53

PRAY GOD'S WORD
Prayer Templates and Acivities /55

- Prayer & Journal Prompts /57
- Prayer Requests /58
- Gratitude Journal /59

Contents
Part II

PART II : INTRODUCTION
(Women of the Bible) / 63

Eve
POWERFUL PURPOSE / 65

Sarah
DAUGHTER OF THE KING / 69

Rebekah
SURRENDERED STRENGTH / 73

Leah
GOD'S KINDNESS IN A MEAN WORLD / 77

Rachel
HOPE IN THE WORLD / 81

Jochebed
COURAGEOUS HOPE / 85

Hannah — A Praying Woman	89
Widow of Zarephath — Death and Resurrection	93
Naomi — A God Who Restores	97
Ruth — Loyalty and Integrity	101
Elizabeth — Rejoice in the Lord	105
Mary — A Mother's Influence	109
Lydia — Nurturing a Welcoming Home	113
List of Positive & Negative Character Qualities	117

Part I

This spiritual growth resource is divided up into three *easy-to-use* sections to offer a systematic approach to Bible study, to growing in faith and deepening your relationship with God.

SECTION 1
Read
God's Word

You can read the Bible, even as a beginner! Let the five Bible reading plans in this toolkit guide you to a starting point for a thriving quiet time.

SECTION 2
Apply
God's Word

Enhance your Scripture reading by choosing a Bible study method or spiritual growth activity from this toolkit to help you understand and process what read in God's Word.

These activities are designed to help you make Scripture an active and meaningful part of your life. The more you think through and meditate on God's Word, the more God's truth will take root in your heart and life.

SECTION 3
Pray
God's Word

You can read the Bible, even as a beginner! Let the five Bible reading plans in this toolkit guide you to a starting point for a thriving quiet time.

SECTION 1
READ
God's Word

This section includes five Bible reading plans to help you read God's Word with confidence, instead of wondering where to start or what to read.

These Scripture guides include:

Foundations of Faith Bible Reading Plan

A journey through some of the most foundational Scriptures to guide you towards a firm understanding of the key elements of our faith.

Heroes of the Bible

Explore the lives of some godly men and women of the Bible and discover how God uses imperfect people for His glory.

The Character of God Bible Reading Plan

Discover the steadfast character of God and explore HIs faithful love to His children. You'll celebrate God's goodness and rejoice how His love rescued and redeemed a flawed mankind!

The Life of Jesus Bible Reading Plan

Explore the prophecies, birth, life, death, and resurrection of Jesus. Learn how God's Scripture promises of the Messiah were completely fulfilled in Jesus.

Books of the Bible Reading Plan

Use this checklist of the books of the Bible to read through the Bible at your own pace. Simply check off when you read each chapter and keep track of your time in God's Word.

Which plan should I start with?

If you're new to Bible study, you don't have to be intimidated. All of these Bible reading plans will guide you towards a vibrant time in God's Word.

As a beginner

You will benefit from starting with the Foundations of Faith Bible Reading Plan. This plan will help you learn and explore crucial Scriptures which discuss key elements to the Christian faith. It will help you understand creation, the sin nature of people, and how God rescued His children through the grace of Jesus. Plus, it gives insight to God's commands for how children of God are to live and act.

For the Bible study veteran

Consider reading through the Books of the Bible reading plan and set a goal to read through the entire Bible. This Scripture guide will help you keep track of what you've read and encourage you to keep going until you're finished.

If you're not sure where to start, consider reading through the Gospels (Matthew, Mark, Luke, and John) to explore and get to know the life of Jesus.

How much should I read each day?

Each Bible reading plan varies in length and the amount of Scripture suggested to read each day.

If you are reading a shorter Scripture of the day, feel free to read more than one day's suggested reading at a time.

If you are reading a plan that has more Scripture than you have time for that day, feel free to stop and mark your place.

While it's up to you how long you spend reading the Bible, **the goal is for you to have time to read Scripture, apply the Bible to your life through an activity, and have time for prayer.** However, if life happens and you can't seem to fit it all in, give yourself grace.

Honestly, some time in God's Word is better than no time in God's Word!

How should I structure my quiet time?

Bible Study

Read a portion of one of the included Bible reading plans.

Activity

Use one of the Bible study method templates or activities designed to help you process and think through the Scripture you just read. Your goal is to think through the details of what you just read and how you can apply it to your life. If you're short on time, use the *25 Questions to Help You Study God's Word with Confidence* to help you retain these concepts and meditate on Truth throughout the day.

Prayer

Spend time being still before God and listening for His voice. Use this time to share your heart with Him, as well as praise Him for HIs faithfulness and many blessings.

SECTION 2
Apply
God's Word

As you begin reading the Bible, it's important to **let Truth take root in your heart.** It's in that time of reading and applying to Scripture to your life where God's Word becomes a cornerstone in your life and your ultimate guidebook in all situations.

It's through meditating on His Word and reminding yourself of Truth where real-life change begins to take root.

How to use these Bible study methods and activities

This toolkit offers a variety of Bible study methods and practical ways to apply God's Word to your life.As you start with this resource, choose one or two activities to use in your quiet time.

Choose an activity based on the time you have and on your activity preference. It's perfectly alright to find activities you love and stick to those few. And it's also alright to rotate through activities and Bible study methods to experience a variety of activities.

The choice is completely up to you!

Bible Study Methods

Topical Study

A Topical Bible study is the perfect way to explore a certain topic of the Bible in depth. As you begin your study, first choose a word/ topic to research, such as prayer. Then look up the word in a Topical Bible or use Biblegateway.com to search for verses on your topic.

This Bible study template has two sections. The first template has frames for you to record and write out your favorite verses on the topic.

After recording the verses, answer the questions on the next page to process and understand your time in God's Word and how His Scriptures connect together.

Verse Mapping

Verse Mapping is a Bible study technique that helps you dissect a verse for further understanding. First, write out the entire verse and then list the translation. Next, choose words from the verse to investigate further. Look up the definition and the synonyms in a dictionary (or at Dictionary.com) and record it on the template.

Then, research and record the verses before and after the original verse on the template. (Example: If you were mapping John 3:16, you would record John 3:15 and John 3:17). Next, using another translation of the Bible, note the similarities and differences between the two translations. Finally, make a plan for how you can apply these verses to your life in the 'Application' section of the template.

Bible Study for Women: *Made Amazingly Simple*

Write the Word

The Write the Word template helps you dissect passages of Scripture and offers further understanding as you look deeper into a passage. First, write out the entire Scripture verses in the section for 'Passage'. Then take notes in each of the sections about the verse(s). The application portion at the end is for you to reflect and apply what you learned through the verse(s).

Book of the Bible Study

This template is perfect for a longer, in-depth study of a particular book in the Bible. Print off a template for each chapter of the book you wish to study, and then use it to record your discoveries while reading.

After reading the chapter, use the template to record any confusing or interesting words in the chapter. Look up the definition and synonyms of the word and record the answers on the template. Then, simply work through each box and record your findings on both pages. (Please note, this template has two pages).

READ Bible Study Method

This simple form can be used as a quick way to record what you read in your Bible. Simply write your answers in each box as a reminder of the passage you read. The READ Bible Study Method is a great tool for those in need of a simple way to track what they are learning in their quiet time. This is also a great method when you're short on time but still want to spend time in God's Word.

My Anchor Verses

Over the years I have filled countless notebooks with my favorite Scriptures, which inspired the My Anchor Verses template. As you come across a verse that encourages, inspires and impacts your life, record it on this page. As you fill up one page, simply print another and keep them together for times when you need to remember the faithfulness of God. It's a blessing to have easy access to your favorite verses in times of need

GRACE Bible Study Method

Let the GRACE Bible study method help you understand and appreciate God's character. It helps you focus on what God has commanded and encourages you to spend time praising God for who He is and all that He has done!

Character Study

Get to know Bible heroes and the people in God's Word by doing a character study. This study will help you understand how each person is a part of God's plan and explore godly character traits. You'll learn important life lessons from the flawed people that God used as a part of His rescue plan for humanity. It's a blessing to see how God used imperfect people to share hope with the world! .

25 Questions to Help You Study God's Word with Confidence

As you study the Bible, use this list of questions to help you process and understand what you read. These questions can be written down or used to help you think through a passage.

Sermon Notes

Use the Sermon Notes template to help you make the most of each sermon and apply it to your life. It even includes a section for you to illustrate (doodle) the message. May this sermon note template guide you to a more meaningful time learning about the Lord.

SECTION 3
PRAY
God's Word

Gratitude journal

Celebrate God's faithfulness through daily gratitude! Use the gratitude journal template to create an attitude of gratitude and thank God for His many blessings.

Prayer and journal prompts

Jump start your prayer life through this calendar of prayer and journal prompts. May these prayer prompts help you pray war room prayers and make your quiet time more meaningful.

Prayer Request Journal

One way to grow deeper in faith is through prayer and talking to God on a regular basis. The Prayer Request Journal template can be used daily, weekly or monthly to record prayers and praises. Keep your Prayer Request Journal sheets throughout the year as a tangible remembrance of what God has done in your life and the lives of others.

MEMO

DATE:

1 READ God's Word

BIBLE READING PLANS

The Life of Jesus
BIBLE READING PLAN

The PROMISE of JESUS

- ☐ GENESIS 3:1-24
- ☐ GENESIS 17:1-22
- ☐ 1 SAMUEL 2:10, ECCLESIASTES 12:14, PSALM 96:10-13
- ☐ PS. 89:3, JEREMIAH 23:5, LUKE 1:32
- ☐ ISAIAH 53:7-12
- ☐ ROMANS 5:6-11
- ☐ ISAIAH 53:4-6. 1 PETER 2:24, 1 PETER 3:18, 1 JOHN 2:2

The LIFE & MINISTRY of JESUS

- ☐ LUKE 2:41-51
- ☐ MATTHEW 3:13-17
- ☐ MATTHEW 4:1-11
- ☐ LUKE 5:1-11
- ☐ JOHN 2:1-11
- ☐ JOHN 6:1-14
- ☐ LUKE 8:40-56

DEATH of JESUS & the PROMISE of ETERNITY with GOD

- ☐ JOHN 12:37-42, LUKE 22:1-5
- ☐ LUKE 22:7-23
- ☐ LUKE 22:39-46
- ☐ LUKE 22:47-62
- ☐ MATTHEW 27:11-31
- ☐ LUKE 23:26-43
- ☐ LUKE 23:44-56
- ☐ LUKE 24:1-12
- ☐ LUKE 24:13-48
- ☐ JOHN 3:16, ROMANS 6:22-23

The BIRTH of JESUS

- ☐ LUKE 1:26-38
- ☐ MATTHEW 1:18-25
- ☐ LUKE 2:1-7
- ☐ LUKE 2:8-20
- ☐ MATTHEW 2:1-12
- ☐ MATTHEW 2:13-23
- ☐ ISAIAH 9:6

Exploring the Character of God

BIBLE READING PLAN

- ☐ EPHESIANS 1:11
- ☐ ROMANS 11:36
- ☐ 1 CORINTHIANS 13
- ☐ ROMANS 5:5-8
- ☐ 1 JOHN 1:9
- ☐ 1 CORINTHIANS 1:9
- ☐ 1 KINGS 8:27
- ☐ JOB 11:7-9
- ☐ PSALM 145:17
- ☐ EPHESIANS 4:7
- ☐ JAMES 1:17
- ☐ EXODUS 34:6-7
- ☐ ACTS 15:18
- ☐ EZEKIEL 11:5
- ☐ HEBREWS 13:8
- ☐ PSALM 102:12
- ☐ ISAIAH 9:6
- ☐ 1 CORINTHIANS 8:6
- ☐ HEBREWS 4:16
- ☐ TITUS 3:5
- ☐ GENESIS 14:19
- ☐ ROMANS 9:15
- ☐ JOHN 5:26
- ☐ 2 CORINTHIANS 3:5
- ☐ 1 SAMUEL 2:2
- ☐ REVELATION 4:8
- ☐ ROMANS 11:33
- ☐ JAMES 1:5
- ☐ GENESIS 18:25
- ☐ PSALM 99:4

Bible Heroes

BIBLE READING PLAN

NOAH
- [ ] GENESIS 6: 5-14
- [ ] GENESIS 6: 15-22
- [ ] GENESIS 7: 1-5
- [ ] GENESIS 7: 6-12
- [ ] GENESIS 7: 13-24
- [ ] GENESIS 8: 1-12
- [ ] GENESIS 8: 13-22

ABRAHAM
- [ ] GENESIS 12: 1-9
- [ ] GENESIS 12: 10-20
- [ ] GENESIS 13: 1-9
- [ ] GENESIS 13: 10-18
- [ ] GENESIS 14: 1-12
- [ ] GENESIS 14: 13-24
- [ ] GENESIS 15: 1-10
- [ ] GENESIS 15: 11-20
- [ ] GENESIS 16: 1-9
- [ ] GENESIS 16: 10-16
- [ ] GENESIS 17: 1-14
- [ ] GENESIS 17: 15-27
- [ ] GENESIS 18: 1-15
- [ ] GENESIS 18: 16-33
- [ ] GENESIS 21: 1-20
- [ ] GENESIS 21: 21-34
- [ ] GENESIS 22: 1-8
- [ ] GENESIS 22: 9-19

JOSEPH
- [ ] GENESIS 37:1-11
- [ ] GENESIS 37: 12-24
- [ ] GENESIS 37: 25-36
- [ ] GENESIS 39: 1-12
- [ ] GENESIS 39: 13-23
- [ ] GENESIS 40: 1-11
- [ ] GENESIS 40: 12-23
- [ ] GENESIS 41: 1-14
- [ ] GENESIS 41: 15-32
- [ ] GENESIS 41: 33-40
- [ ] GENESIS 41: 41-57
- [ ] GENESIS 42: 1-17
- [ ] GENESIS 42: 18-38
- [ ] GENESIS 43: 1-16
- [ ] GENESIS 43: 17-34
- [ ] GENESIS 44: 1-13
- [ ] GENESIS 44: 14-34
- [ ] GENESIS 45: 1-15
- [ ] GENESIS 45: 16-28
- [ ] GENESIS 46: 1-7
- [ ] GENESIS 46: 26-34
- [ ] GENESIS 47: 1-12
- [ ] GENESIS 47: 13-31

Bible Heroes

BIBLE READING PLAN

MOSES

- ☐ EXODUS 1: 6-22
- ☐ EXODUS 2: 1-10
- ☐ EXODUS 2: 11-25
- ☐ EXODUS 3: 1-10
- ☐ EXODUS 3: 11-21
- ☐ EXODUS 4: 1-17
- ☐ EXODUS 4: 18-31
- ☐ EXODUS 5: 1-9
- ☐ EXODUS 5: 10-23
- ☐ EXODUS 6: 1-15
- ☐ EXODUS 6: 16-30
- ☐ EXODUS 7: 1-12
- ☐ EXODUS 7: 13-25
- ☐ EXODUS 8: 1-15
- ☐ EXODUS 8: 15-32
- ☐ EXODUS 9: 1-12
- ☐ EXODUS 9: 13-35
- ☐ EXODUS 10: 1-15
- ☐ EXODUS 10: 16-29
- ☐ EXODUS 11
- ☐ EXODUS 12: 1-13
- ☐ EXODUS 12: 14-30
- ☐ EXODUS 12: 31-42
- ☐ EXODUS 12: 43-51
- ☐ EXODUS 13: 1-16
- ☐ EXODUS 13: 17-22
- ☐ EXODUS 14: 1-14
- ☐ EXODUS 14: 15-31
- ☐ EXODUS 15: 1-19
- ☐ EXODUS 15: 20-27
- ☐ EXODUS 16: 1-16
- ☐ EXODUS 16: 17-36
- ☐ EXODUS 17
- ☐ EXODUS 18: 1-16
- ☐ EXODUS 18: 17-27
- ☐ EXODUS 19: 1-15
- ☐ EXODUS 19: 16-25
- ☐ EXODUS 20: 1-15
- ☐ EXODUS 20: 16-26
- ☐ EXODUS 24
- ☐ EXODUS 25: 1-9
- ☐ EXODUS 31: 12-18
- ☐ EXODUS 32: 1-16
- ☐ EXODUS 32: 17-35
- ☐ EXODUS 33: 1-13
- ☐ EXODUS 33: 14-23
- ☐ EXODUS 34: 1-17
- ☐ EXODUS 34: 18-35
- ☐ EXODUS 35: 1-17
- ☐ EXODUS 35: 18-35
- ☐ EXODUS 36: 1-17
- ☐ EXODUS 36: 18-38
- ☐ EXODUS 39: 32-43
- ☐ EXODUS 40: 1-19
- ☐ EXODUS 40: 20-38

Bible Heroes
BIBLE READING PLAN

MOSES

- ☐ NUMBERS 1: 1-18
- ☐ NUMBERS 1: 19-37
- ☐ NUMBERS 1: 38-54
- ☐ NUMBERS 2: 1-17
- ☐ NUMBERS 2: 18-34
- ☐ NUMBERS 3: 1-16
- ☐ NUMBERS 3: 17-34
- ☐ NUMBERS 3: 35-50
- ☐ NUMBERS 5: 1-16
- ☐ NUMBERS 5: 17-30
- ☐ NUMBERS 9: 1-12
- ☐ NUMBERS 9: 13-23
- ☐ NUMBERS 10: 1-18
- ☐ NUMBERS 10: 19-36
- ☐ NUMBERS 11: 1-17
- ☐ NUMBERS 11: 18-35
- ☐ NUMBERS 12
- ☐ NUMBERS 13: 1-16
- ☐ NUMBERS 13: 17-33
- ☐ NUMBERS 14: 1-22
- ☐ NUMBERS 14: 23-45
- ☐ NUMBERS 15: 1-20
- ☐ NUMBERS 15: 21-41
- ☐ NUMBERS 16: 1-17
- ☐ NUMBERS 16: 18-35
- ☐ NUMBERS 16: 35-50
- ☐ NUMBERS 17
- ☐ NUMBERS 18: 1-16
- ☐ NUMBERS 18: 17-32
- ☐ NUMBERS 20: 1-14
- ☐ NUMBERS 20: 15-29
- ☐ NUMBERS 21: 1-17
- ☐ NUMBERS 21: 35
- ☐ NUMBERS 22: 1-21
- ☐ NUMBERS 22: 22-41
- ☐ NUMBERS 23: 1-15
- ☐ NUMBERS 23: 16-30
- ☐ NUMBERS 24: 1-13
- ☐ NUMBERS 24: 14-25
- ☐ NUMBERS 25
- ☐ NUMBERS 26: 1-22
- ☐ NUMBERS 26: 23-45
- ☐ NUMBERS 26: 45-65
- ☐ NUMBERS 27
- ☐ NUMBERS 28: 1-15
- ☐ NUMBERS 28: 16-31
- ☐ NUMBERS 29: 1-20
- ☐ NUMBERS 29: 21-40
- ☐ NUMBERS 30
- ☐ NUMBERS 31: 1-18
- ☐ NUMBERS 31: 19-37
- ☐ NUMBERS 31: 38-54
- ☐ NUMBERS 32: 1-21
- ☐ NUMBERS 32: 22- 42

Bible Heroes
BIBLE READING PLAN

MOSES

- ☐ NUMBERS 33: 1-19
- ☐ NUMBERS 33: 20-39
- ☐ NUMBERS 33: 40-56
- ☐ NUMBERS 34: 1-14
- ☐ NUMBERS 34: 15-29
- ☐ NUMBERS 35: 1-17
- ☐ NUMBERS 35: 18-34
- ☐ NUMBERS 36
- ☐ DEUTERONOMY 1: 1-23
- ☐ DEUTERONOMY 1: 24-46
- ☐ DEUTERONOMY 2: 1-17
- ☐ DEUTERONOMY 2: 18-37
- ☐ DEUTERONOMY 3: 1-15
- ☐ DEUTERONOMY 3: 16-29
- ☐ DEUTERONOMY 4: 1-17
- ☐ DEUTERONOMY 4: 18-25
- ☐ DEUTERONOMY 4: 26-49
- ☐ DEUTERONOMY 5: 1-16
- ☐ DEUTERONOMY 5: 17-33
- ☐ DEUTERONOMY 6: 1-13
- ☐ DEUTERONOMY 6: 14-25
- ☐ DEUTERONOMY 7: 1-13
- ☐ DEUTERONOMY 7: 14-26
- ☐ DEUTERONOMY 8
- ☐ DEUTERONOMY 9: 1-14
- ☐ DEUTERONOMY 9: 15-29
- ☐ DEUTERONOMY 10
- ☐ DEUTERONOMY 11: 1-16
- ☐ DEUTERONOMY 11: 17-32
- ☐ DEUTERONOMY 27: 1-13
- ☐ DEUTERONOMY 27: 14-26
- ☐ DEUTERONOMY 29: 1-15
- ☐ DEUTERONOMY 29: 16-29
- ☐ DEUTERONOMY 30
- ☐ DEUTERONOMY 31: 1-15
- ☐ DEUTERONOMY 31: 16-30
- ☐ DEUTERONOMY 32: 1-18
- ☐ DEUTERONOMY 32: 19-37
- ☐ DEUTERONOMY 32: 38-52
- ☐ DEUTERONOMY 33: 1-15
- ☐ DEUTERONOMY 33: 16-29
- ☐ DEUTERONOMY 34: 1-12

JOSHUA

- ☐ JOSHUA 1: 1-9
- ☐ JOSHUA 1: 10-18
- ☐ JOSHUA 2: 1-12
- ☐ JOSHUA 2: 13-24
- ☐ JOSHUA 3: 1-8
- ☐ JOSHUA 3: 9-17
- ☐ JOSHUA 4: 1-12
- ☐ JOSHUA 4: 13-24
- ☐ JOSHUA 5
- ☐ JOSHUA 6: 1-14
- ☐ JOSHUA 6: 15-27

Bible Heroes

BIBLE READING PLAN

NAOMI & RUTH
- ☐ RUTH 1: 1-10
- ☐ RUTH 1: 11-22
- ☐ RUTH 2: 1-11
- ☐ RUTH 2:12-23
- ☐ RUTH 3
- ☐ RUTH 4:1-16

HANNAH
- ☐ SAMUEL 1: 1-11
- ☐ SAMUEL 1: 12-20
- ☐ SAMUEL 1: 21-28
- ☐ SAMUEL 2: 1-11

SAMUEL
- ☐ 1 SAMUEL 2: 12-26
- ☐ 1 SAMUEL 2: 27-36
- ☐ 1 SAMUEL 3: 1-14
- ☐ 1 SAMUEL 3: 15-21
- ☐ 1 SAMUEL 4: 1-11
- ☐ 1 SAMUEL 4: 12-22
- ☐ 1 SAMUEL 5
- ☐ 1 SAMUEL 6: 1-12
- ☐ 1 SAMUEL 6: 13-21
- ☐ 1 SAMUEL 7

DAVID
- ☐ 1 SAMUEL 16: 1-13
- ☐ 1 SAMUEL 16: 14-25
- ☐ 1 SAMUEL 17: 26-40
- ☐ 1 SAMUEL 17: 41-58
- ☐ 1 SAMUEL 18: 1-11
- ☐ 1 SAMUEL 18: 12-30
- ☐ 1 SAMUEL 19: 1-12
- ☐ 1 SAMUEL 19: 13-24
- ☐ 1 SAMUEL 20: 1-23
- ☐ 1 SAMUEL 20: 24-42
- ☐ 1 SAMUEL 21
- ☐ 1 SAMUEL 22: 1-10
- ☐ 1 SAMUEL 22: 11-23
- ☐ 1 SAMUEL 23: 1-14
- ☐ 1 SAMUEL 23: 15-29
- ☐ 1 SAMUEL 24
- ☐ 1 SAMUEL 25: 1-22
- ☐ 1 SAMUEL 25: 23-44
- ☐ 1 SAMUEL 26: 1-14
- ☐ 1 SAMUEL 26: 15-25
- ☐ 1 SAMUEL 27
- ☐ 1 SAMUEL 28
- ☐ 1 SAMUEL 29
- ☐ 1 SAMUEL 30: 1-15
- ☐ 1 SAMUEL 30: 16-30
- ☐ 1 SAMUEL 31

Bible Heroes

BIBLE READING PLAN

DAVID (cont...)

- ☐ 2 SAMUEL 1: 1-15
- ☐ 2 SAMUEL 1: 16-27
- ☐ 2 SAMUEL 2: 1-14
- ☐ 2 SAMUEL 2: 15-32
- ☐ 2 SAMUEL 5: 1-15
- ☐ 2 SAMUEL 5: 16-25
- ☐ 2 SAMUEL 6: 1-11
- ☐ 2 SAMUEL 6: 12-23
- ☐ 2 SAMUEL 7
- ☐ 2 SAMUEL 8
- ☐ 2 SAMUEL 9
- ☐ 2 SAMUEL 10
- ☐ 2 SAMUEL 11: 1-13
- ☐ 2 SAMUEL 11: 14-27
- ☐ 2 SAMUEL 12: 1-15
- ☐ 2 SAMUEL 12: 16-31
- ☐ 2 SAMUEL 13: 1-20
- ☐ 2 SAMUEL 13: 21-39
- ☐ 2 SAMUEL 14: 1-16
- ☐ 2 SAMUEL 14: 17-33
- ☐ 2 SAMUEL 15: 1-17
- ☐ 2 SAMUEL 15: 18-27
- ☐ 2 SAMUEL 16: 1-16
- ☐ 2 SAMUEL 16: 17-23
- ☐ 2 SAMUEL 17: 1-15
- ☐ 2 SAMUEL 17: 16-29
- ☐ 2 SAMUEL 18: 1-16
- ☐ 2 SAMUEL 18: 17-33
- ☐ 2 SAMUEL 19: 1-21
- ☐ 2 SAMUEL 19: 22-43
- ☐ 2 SAMUEL 20: 1-13
- ☐ 2 SAMUEL 20: 14-26
- ☐ 2 SAMUEL 21
- ☐ 2 SAMUEL 22: 1-25
- ☐ 2 SAMUEL 22: 26-51
- ☐ 2 SAMUEL 23: 1-20
- ☐ 2 SAMUEL 23: 21-39
- ☐ 2 SAMUEL 24: 1-12
- ☐ 2 SAMUEL 24: 13-24
- ☐ 1 KINGS 1: 1-26
- ☐ 1 KINGS 1: 27-53
- ☐ 1 KINGS 2: 1-12

NEHEMIAH

- ☐ NEHEMIAH 1
- ☐ NEHEMIAH 2: 1-10
- ☐ NEHEMIAH 2: 11-20
- ☐ NEHEMIAH 3: 1-16
- ☐ NEHEMIAH 3: 17-32
- ☐ NEHEMIAH 4: 1-12
- ☐ NEHEMIAH 4: 13-23
- ☐ NEHEMIAH 5
- ☐ NEHEMIAH 6
- ☐ NEHEMIAH 7: 1-6, 64-73
- ☐ NEHEMIAH 8

Bible Heroes
BIBLE READING PLAN

NEHEMIAH (cont...)
- ☐ NEHEMIAH 9: 1-18
- ☐ NEHEMIAH 9: 19-38
- ☐ NEHEMIAH 10: 1-20
- ☐ NEHEMIAH 10: 20-39
- ☐ NEHEMIAH 11: 1-4, 20-36
- ☐ NEHEMIAH 12: 1-21
- ☐ NEHEMIAH 12: 22-47
- ☐ NEHEMIAH 13: 1-15
- ☐ NEHEMIAH 13: 16-31

ESTHER
- ☐ ESTHER 1: 1-11
- ☐ ESTHER 1: 12-22
- ☐ ESTHER 2: 1-14
- ☐ ESTHER 2: 15-23
- ☐ ESTHER 3
- ☐ ESTHER 4
- ☐ ESTHER 5
- ☐ ESTHER 6
- ☐ ESTHER 7
- ☐ ESTHER 8
- ☐ ESTHER 9: 1-15
- ☐ ESTHER 9: 16-32
- ☐ ESTHER 10

JEREMIAH
- ☐ JEREMIAH 1
- ☐ JEREMIAH 2: 1-17
- ☐ JEREMIAH 2: 18-37
- ☐ JEREMIAH 3: 1-13
- ☐ JEREMIAH 3: 14-25
- ☐ JEREMIAH 4: 1-15
- ☐ JEREMIAH 4: 16-31
- ☐ JEREMIAH 5: 1-17
- ☐ JEREMIAH 5: 18-31
- ☐ JEREMIAH 6: 1-15
- ☐ JEREMIAH 6: 16-30
- ☐ JEREMIAH 7: 1-15
- ☐ JEREMIAH 7: 16-34
- ☐ JEREMIAH 8: 1-11
- ☐ JEREMIAH 8: 12-22
- ☐ JEREMIAH 9: 1-13
- ☐ JEREMIAH 9: 14-26
- ☐ JEREMIAH 10: 1-16
- ☐ JEREMIAH 10: 17-25
- ☐ JEREMIAH 11
- ☐ JEREMIAH 12
- ☐ JEREMIAH 13: 1-13
- ☐ JEREMIAH 13: 14-27
- ☐ JEREMIAH 14
- ☐ JEREMIAH 15

Bible Heroes

BIBLE READING PLAN

JEREMIAH (cont...)

- ☐ JEREMIAH 16
- ☐ JEREMIAH 17: 1-13
- ☐ JEREMIAH 17: 14-27
- ☐ JEREMIAH 18: 1-12
- ☐ JEREMIAH 18: 13-23
- ☐ JEREMIAH 19
- ☐ JEREMIAH 20
- ☐ JEREMIAH 21
- ☐ JEREMIAH 22: 1-15
- ☐ JEREMIAH 22: 16-30
- ☐ JEREMIAH 23: 1-20
- ☐ JEREMIAH 23: 21-40
- ☐ JEREMIAH 24
- ☐ JEREMIAH 25: 1-18
- ☐ JEREMIAH 25: 19-38
- ☐ JEREMIAH 26: 1-12
- ☐ JEREMIAH 26: 13-24
- ☐ JEREMIAH 27
- ☐ JEREMIAH 28
- ☐ JEREMIAH 29: 1-16
- ☐ JEREMIAH 29: 17-30
- ☐ JEREMIAH 30: 1-12
- ☐ JEREMIAH 30: 13-24
- ☐ JEREMIAH 31: 1-20
- ☐ JEREMIAH 31: 21-40
- ☐ JEREMIAH 32: 1-22
- ☐ JEREMIAH 32: 23-44
- ☐ JEREMIAH 33: 1-13
- ☐ JEREMIAH 33: 14-26
- ☐ JEREMIAH 34: 1-11
- ☐ JEREMIAH 34: 12-22
- ☐ JEREMIAH 35
- ☐ JEREMIAH 36: 1-16
- ☐ JEREMIAH 36: 17-32
- ☐ JEREMIAH 37: 1-10
- ☐ JEREMIAH 37: 11-21
- ☐ JEREMIAH 38: 1-14
- ☐ JEREMIAH 38: 15-28
- ☐ JEREMIAH 39
- ☐ JEREMIAH 40
- ☐ JEREMIAH 41
- ☐ JEREMIAH 42: 1-10
- ☐ JEREMIAH 42: 11-22
- ☐ JEREMIAH 43
- ☐ JEREMIAH 44: 1-15
- ☐ JEREMIAH 44: 16-30
- ☐ JEREMIAH 45
- ☐ JEREMIAH 46: 1-14
- ☐ JEREMIAH 46: 15-28
- ☐ JEREMIAH 47
- ☐ JEREMIAH 48: 1-23
- ☐ JEREMIAH 48: 24-47
- ☐ JEREMIAH 49: 1-19
- ☐ JEREMIAH 49: 20-39
- ☐ JEREMIAH 50: 1-23
- ☐ JEREMIAH 50: 24-46

Bible Heroes
BIBLE READING PLAN

JEREMIAH (cont...)
- ☐ JEREMIAH 51: 1-21
- ☐ JEREMIAH 51: 22-42
- ☐ JEREMIAH 51: 43-64
- ☐ JEREMIAH 52: 1-17
- ☐ JEREMIAH 52: 18-54

DANIEL
- ☐ DANIEL 1: 1-14
- ☐ DANIEL 1: 15-21
- ☐ DANIEL 2: 1-23
- ☐ DANIEL 2: 24-49
- ☐ DANIEL 3: 1-15
- ☐ DANIEL 3: 16-30
- ☐ DANIEL 4: 1-18
- ☐ DANIEL 4: 19-37
- ☐ DANIEL 5: 1-16
- ☐ DANIEL 5: 17-31
- ☐ DANIEL 6: 1-14
- ☐ DANIEL 6: 15-28
- ☐ DANIEL 7: 1-14
- ☐ DANIEL 7: 15-28
- ☐ DANIEL 8: 1-14
- ☐ DANIEL 8: 15-27
- ☐ DANIEL 9: 1-14
- ☐ DANIEL 9: 15-27
- ☐ DANIEL 10: 1-10
- ☐ DANIEL 10: 11-21
- ☐ DANIEL 11: 1-22
- ☐ DANIEL 11: 23-45
- ☐ DANIEL 12

JOHN THE BAPTIST
- ☐ LUKE 1: 1-10
- ☐ LUKE 1: 11-25
- ☐ LUKE 1: 57-66
- ☐ LUKE 1: 67-80
- ☐ LUKE 3: 1-20
- ☐ JOHN 1: 1-18
- ☐ JOHN 1: 19-34
- ☐ MATTHEW 3: 1-17
- ☐ JOHN 3: 22-36
- ☐ MATTHEW 11: 1-19
- ☐ MATTHEW 14: 1-12

MARY & JOSEPH
- ☐ LUKE 1: 26-32
- ☐ LUKE 1: 39-56
- ☐ LUKE 2: 1-21
- ☐ MATTHEW 1: 18-25
- ☐ MATTHEW 2: 13-23
- ☐ JOHN 2: 1-2
- ☐ JOHN 19: 17-27

Bible Heroes

BIBLE READING PLAN

PETER
- [ ] LUKE 5: 1-11
- [ ] LUKE 6: 12-16, LUKE 9: 18-20
- [ ] MATTHEW 14: 22-34
- [ ] MATTHEW 16: 13-20
- [ ] MATTHEW 17: 1-13
- [ ] MATTHEW 18: 21-35
- [ ] MATTHEW 19: 31-46
- [ ] MATTHEW 26: 1-16
- [ ] MATTHEW 26: 17-30
- [ ] MATTHEW 26: 31-46
- [ ] JOHN 18: 1-15
- [ ] JOHN 18: 16-27
- [ ] JOHN 21: 1-14
- [ ] JOHN 21: 15-25
- [ ] ACTS 2: 1-15
- [ ] ACTS 2: 16-30
- [ ] ACTS 2: 31-47
- [ ] ACTS 3: 1-13
- [ ] ACTS 3: 14-26
- [ ] ACTS 4: 1-16
- [ ] ACTS 4: 17-27
- [ ] ACTS 5: 1-21
- [ ] ACTS 5: 22-42
- [ ] ACTS 10: 1-23
- [ ] ACTS 10: 24-48
- [ ] ACTS 11: 1-15
- [ ] ACTS 11: 16-30
- [ ] ACTS 12: 1-19
- [ ] ACTS 12: 20-25

STEPHEN
- [ ] ACTS 6
- [ ] ACTS 7: 1-19
- [ ] ACTS 7: 20-38
- [ ] ACTS 7: 39-60

PAUL
- [ ] ACTS 9: 1-19
- [ ] ACTS 9: 20-43
- [ ] ACTS 13: 1-20
- [ ] ACTS 13: 21-39
- [ ] ACTS 13: 40-52
- [ ] ACTS 14: 1-14
- [ ] ACTS 14: 15-28
- [ ] ACTS 15: 1-20
- [ ] ACTS 15: 21-41
- [ ] ACTS 16: 1-20
- [ ] ACTS 16: 21-40
- [ ] ACTS 17: 1-17
- [ ] ACTS 17: 18-34
- [ ] ACTS 18: 1-14
- [ ] ACTS 18: 15-28

Bible Heroes

BIBLE READING PLAN

PAUL (cont...)

- [ ] ACTS 19: 1-20
- [ ] ACTS 19: 21-41
- [ ] ACTS 20: 1-18
- [ ] ACTS 20: 19-38
- [ ] ACTS 21: 1-20
- [ ] ACTS 21: 21-40
- [ ] ACTS 22: 1-15
- [ ] ACTS 22: 16-30
- [ ] ACTS 23: 1:17
- [ ] ACTS 23: 18-34
- [ ] ACTS 24: 1-13
- [ ] ACTS 24: 14-27
- [ ] ACTS 25: 1-13
- [ ] ACTS 25: 14-27
- [ ] ACTS 26: 1-16
- [ ] ACTS 26: 17-32
- [ ] ACTS 27: 1-22
- [ ] ACTS 27: 23-44
- [ ] ACTS 28: 1-15
- [ ] ACTS 28: 16-31

TIMOTHY

- [ ] 1 THESSALONIANS 1
- [ ] 1 THESSALONIANS 2
- [ ] 1 THESSALONIANS 3
- [ ] 1 TIMOTHY 1
- [ ] 1 TIMOTHY 2
- [ ] 1 TIMOTHY 3
- [ ] 1 TIMOTHY 4
- [ ] 1 TIMOTHY 5
- [ ] 1 TIMOTHY 6
- [ ] 2 TIMOTHY 1
- [ ] 2 TIMOTHY 2: 1-13
- [ ] 2 TIMOTHY 2: 14-26
- [ ] 2 TIMOTHY 3
- [ ] 2 TIMOTHY 4

FOR FURTHER READING ON PAUL, READ HIS LETTERS IN THE BOOK OF ROMANS, I & II CORINTHIANS, GALATIANS, EPHESIANS, PHILIPPIANS, COLOSSIANS, I & II THESSALONIANS, I & II TIMOTHY, TITUS, AND PHILEMON.

Foundations of Faith

BIBLE READING PLAN

GOD
- ISAIAH 44:6-8
- PSALM 97:9
- REVELATION 22:13
- DEUTERONOMY 32:4, 2 SAMUEL 22:31
- JAMES 1:17
- JOHN 4:24
- PSALM 147:5
- REVELATION 4:8
- DEUTERONOMY 6:4, JEREMIAH 10:10
- ACTS 17:24
- PSALM 8:1, PSALM 96:4
- 1 SAMUEL 2:2
- NUMBERS 23:19
- PSALM 89:14, PSALM 90:2
- EXODUS 34:6
- 1 TIMOTHY 1:17

CREATION
- GENESIS 1:1-15
- GENESIS 1:16-31
- GENESIS 2:1-12
- GENESIS 2:13-25
- HEBREWS 11:3, EXODUS 20:1, ROMANS 4:17

SIN
- GENESIS 2:15-17
- 1 JOHN 3:4
- ROMANS 5:12-14
- ROMANS 3:23
- JAMES 4:17
- 1 JOHN 1:8-10
- ROMANS 6:23

JESUS
- ISAIAH 9:6
- MATTHEW 1:18-25
- MARK 14:61-62
- JOHN 3:16-18
- JOHN 3:34-36
- ISAIAH 53
- ROMANS 5:6-11
- ROMANS 2:13-16
- MATTHEW 20:28
- MATTHEW 26:28
- JOHN 6:51
- JOHN 10:11
- JOHN 10:17
- ROMANS 3:24-25
- 1 PETER 2:24
- 1 PETER 3:18
- 1 JOHN 2:2

Bible Study for Women: *Made Amazingly Simple*

Foundations of Faith

BIBLE READING PLAN

JESUS (cont...)
- ☐ HEBREWS 9:28
- ☐ 1 JOHN 3:16
- ☐ ROMANS 6:9
- ☐ ROMANS 14:9
- ☐ 2 CORINTHIANS 5:21
- ☐ 2 TIMOTHY 1:9
- ☐ MATTHEW 25:31-34

SALVATION
- ☐ ROMANS 5:18-20
- ☐ JOHN 3:16
- ☐ ISAIAH 1:18
- ☐ JOEL 2:32
- ☐ ACTS 4:12
- ☐ ACTS 13:38-39
- ☐ ACTS 16: 30-34
- ☐ 1 CORINTHIANS 6:11
- ☐ 2 TITUS 1:9-10
- ☐ 1 JOHN 4:9-10
- ☐ ACTS 2:38
- ☐ ACTS 3:19
- ☐ JOHN 11:25
- ☐ ROMANS 3:21-26
- ☐ ROMANS 5:1-2
- ☐ GALATIANS 2:15-16
- ☐ EPHESIANS 2:8

THE TRINITY
- ☐ MATTHEW 28:19
- ☐ JOHN 3:34
- ☐ JOHN 14:16
- ☐ JOHN 14:26
- ☐ JOHN 15:26
- ☐ JOHN 16:13
- ☐ ACTS 2:33
- ☐ ROMANS 1;3
- ☐ ROMANS 8:9-11
- ☐ ROMANS 8:26-27
- ☐ TITUS 3:4
- ☐ 2 CORINTHIANS 13:14
- ☐ EPHESIANS 4:4-6
- ☐ 1 PETER 1:2

TEMPTATION
- ☐ 1 CORINTHIANS 10:13
- ☐ MATTHEW 26: 41
- ☐ MATTHEW 4:1-11
- ☐ HEBREWS 2:18
- ☐ HEBREWS 4:15
- ☐ ROMANS 8:35-89
- ☐ JAMES 1:2-4
- ☐ JAMES 1:12
- ☐ 1 PETER 1:6-7
- ☐ PROVERBS 4:14-15
- ☐ ROMANS 6: 12-14
- ☐ 1 PETER 5:8-9

Foundations of Faith

BIBLE READING PLAN

FAITH

- ☐ HEBREWS 11:1-3
- ☐ HEBREWS 11:6
- ☐ PSALM 16: 5-11
- ☐ JOSHUA 1:9
- ☐ PROVERBS 3:5
- ☐ PSALM 13:5
- ☐ PSALM 130:5
- ☐ ISAIAH 12:2
- ☐ JOHN 1:9-13
- ☐ JOHN 3:36
- ☐ JOHN 5:24
- ☐ JOHN 20:31
- ☐ ROMANS 10:10
- ☐ ROMANS 3:22-28
- ☐ ROMANS 5:1

THE BIBLE

- ☐ 2 TIMOTHY 3:14-17
- ☐ PSALM 12:6
- ☐ LUKE 8:4-15
- ☐ EPHESIANS 6:13-17
- ☐ PSALM 119:89
- ☐ MATTHEW 24:35
- ☐ 1 PETER 1:25
- ☐ PSALM 119:103
- ☐ PSALM 119:11
- ☐ JOHN 5:24
- ☐ REVELATION 1:3
- ☐ PROVERBS 30:5
- ☐ MATTHEW 4:4
- ☐ LUKE 11:28
- ☐ 1 THESSALONIANS 2:13
- ☐ HEBREWS 4:12

Foundations of Faith

BIBLE READING PLAN

CHRISTIAN LIVING

- ☐ DEUTERONOMY 6:5
- ☐ DEUTERONOMY 11:1
- ☐ DEUTERONOMY 30:16
- ☐ DEUTERONOMY 10:12
- ☐ JOSHUA 22:5
- ☐ MATTHEW 22:37
- ☐ PSALM 33:18
- ☐ JOHN 13:34-35
- ☐ ROMANS 12:10
- ☐ 2 CORINTHIANS 13:11
- ☐ GALATIANS 5:13
- ☐ LEVITICUS 19:37
- ☐ LEVITICUS 20:8
- ☐ DEUTERONOMY 5:32
- ☐ JOSHUA 22:5
- ☐ ECCLESIASTES 12:13
- ☐ JAMES 1:22
- ☐ JOHN 14:15
- ☐ 1 JOHN 2:3
- ☐ PSALM 143:10
- ☐ JEREMIAH 7:23
- ☐ PROVERBS 2:1-10
- ☐ PROVERBS 9:10-12
- ☐ PSALM 90:12
- ☐ PSALM 111:10
- ☐ PROVERBS 3:1-7
- ☐ ISAIAH 40:28-31
- ☐ ISAIAH 18:30-32
- ☐ PSALM 28:6-9
- ☐ PSALM 59:16-17
- ☐ PSALM 73:23-26
- ☐ ROMANS 5:1-5
- ☐ PSALM 31:24
- ☐ PSALM 33:18-22
- ☐ ISAIAH 40:31
- ☐ JEREMIAH 29:11
- ☐ PROVERBS 3:5-6
- ☐ PSALM 28:7
- ☐ PSALM 37:3
- ☐ ISAIAH 26:4
- ☐ PROVERBS 12:22
- ☐ PHILIPPIANS 4:8
- ☐ PROVERBS 12:17
- ☐ PROVERBS 19:5
- ☐ 1 PETER 4:9-10
- ☐ EPHESIANS 6:7
- ☐ ROMANS 12:13
- ☐ HEBREWS 13:2

OLD TESTAMENT

GENESIS

1 2 3 4 5 6 7 8 9 10
11 12 13 14 15 16 17 18 19 20
21 22 23 24 25 26 27 28 29 30
31 32 33 34 35 36 37 38 39 40
41 42 43 44 45 46 47 48 49 50

EXODUS

1 2 3 4 5 6 7 8 9 10
11 12 13 14 15 16 17 18 19 20
21 22 23 24 25 26 27 28 29 30
31 32 33 34 35 36 37 38 39 40

LEVITICUS

1 2 3 4 5 6 7 8 9 10
11 12 13 14 15 16 17 18 19 20
21 22 23 24 25 26 27

NUMBERS

1 2 3 4 5 6 7 8 9 10
11 12 13 14 15 16 17 18 19 20
21 22 23 24 25 26 27 28 29 30
31 32 33 34 35 36

DEUTERONOMY

1 2 3 4 5 6 7 8 9 10
11 12 13 14 15 16 17 18 19 20
21 22 23 24 25 26 27 28 29 30
31 32 33 34

JOSHUA

1 2 3 4 5 6 7 8 9 10
11 12 13 14 15 16 17 18 19 20
21 22 23 24

JUDGES

1 2 3 4 5 6 7 8 9 10
11 12 13 14 15 16 17 18 19 20
21

RUTH

1 2 3 4

1 SAMUEL

1 2 3 4 5 6 7 8 9 10
11 12 13 14 15 16 17 18 19 20
21 22 23 24 25 26 27 28 29 30
31

2 SAMUEL

1 2 3 4 5 6 7 8 9 10
11 12 13 14 15 16 17 18 19 20
21 22 23 24

1 KINGS

1 2 3 4 5 6 7 8 9 10
11 12 13 14 15 16 17 18 19 20
21 22

2 KINGS

1 2 3 4 5 6 7 8 9 10
11 12 13 14 15 16 17 18 19 20
21 22 23 24 25

Bible Study for Women: *Made Amazingly Simple*

OLD TESTAMENT

1 CHRONICLES

1 2 3 4 5 6 7 8 9 10
11 12 13 14 15 16 17 18 19 20
21 22 23 24 25 26 27 28 29

2 CHRONICLES

1 2 3 4 5 6 7 8 9 10
11 12 13 14 15 16 17 18 19 20
21 22 23 24 25 26 27 28 29 30
31 32 33 34 35 36

EZRA

1 2 3 4 5 6 7 8 9 10

NEHEMIAH

1 2 3 4 5 6 7 8 9 10
11 12 13

ESTHER

1 2 3 4 5 6 7 8 9 10

JOB

1 2 3 4 5 6 7 8 9 10
11 12 13 14 15 16 17 18 19 20
21 22 23 24 25 26 27 28 29 30
31 32 33 34 35 36 37 38 39 40
41 42

PSALMS

1 2 3 4 5 6 7 8 9 10
11 12 13 14 15 16 17 18 19 20
21 22 23 24 25 26 27 28 29 30
31 32 33 34 35 36 37 38 39 40
41 42 43 44 45 46 47 48 49 50
51 52 53 54 55 56 57 58 59 60
61 62 63 64 65 66 67 68 69 70
71 72 73 74 75 76 77 78 79 80
81 82 83 84 85 86 87 88 89 90
91 92 93 94 95 96 97 98 99 100
101 102 103 104 105 106 107 108 109 110
111 112 113 114 115 116 117 118 119 120
121 122 123 124 125 126 127 128 129 130
131 132 133 134 135 136 137 138 139 140
141 142 143 144 145 146 147 148 149 150

PROVERBS

1 2 3 4 5 6 7 8 9 10
11 12 13 14 15 16 17 18 19 20
21 22 23 24 25 26 27 28 29 30
31

ECCLESIASTES

1 2 3 4 5 6 7 8 9 10
11 12

SONG OF SOLOMON

1 2 3 4 5 6 7 8

OLD TESTAMENT

ISAIAH
1 2 3 4 5 6 7 8 9 10
11 12 13 14 15 16 17 18 19 20
21 22 23 24 25 26 27 28 29 30
31 32 33 34 35 36 37 38 39 40
41 42 43 44 45 46 47 48 49 50
51 52 53 54 55 56 57 58 59 60
61 62 63 64 65 66

JEREMIAH
1 2 3 4 5 6 7 8 9 10
11 12 13 14 15 16 17 18 19 20
21 22 23 24 25 26 27 28 29 30
31 32 33 34 35 36 37 38 39 40
41 42 43 44 45 46 47 48 49 50
51 52

LAMENTATIONS
1 2 3 4 5

EZEKIEL
1 2 3 4 5 6 7 8 9 10
11 12 13 14 15 16 17 18 19 20
21 22 23 24 25 26 27 28 29 30
31 32 33 34 35 36 37 38 39 40
41 42 43 44 45 46 47 48

DANIEL
1 2 3 4 5 6 7 8 9 10
11 12

HOSEA
1 2 3 4 5 6 7 8 9 10
11 12 13 14

JOEL
1 2 3

AMOS
1 2 3 4 5 6 7 8 9

OBADIAH
1

JONAH
1 2 3 4

MICAH
1 2 3 4 5 6 7

NAHUM
1 2 3

HABAKKUK
1 2 3

ZEPHANIAH
1 2 3

HAGGAI
1 2

ZECHARIAH
1 2 3 4 5 6 7 8 9 10
11 12 13 14

MALACHI
1 2 3 4

NEW TESTAMENT

MATTHEW
1 2 3 4 5 6 7 8 9 10
11 12 13 14 15 16 17 18 19 20
21 22 23 24 25 26 27 28

MARK
1 2 3 4 5 6 7 8 9 10
11 12 13 14 15 16

LUKE
1 2 3 4 5 6 7 8 9 10
11 12 13 14 15 16 17 18 19 20
21 22 23 24

JOHN
1 2 3 4 5 6 7 8 9 10
11 12 13 14 15 16 17 18 19 20
21

ACTS
1 2 3 4 5 6 7 8 9 10
11 12 13 14 15 16 17 18 19 20
21 22 23 24 25 26 27 28

ROMANS
1 2 3 4 5 6 7 8 9 10
11 12 13 14 15 16

1 CORINTHIANS
1 2 3 4 5 6 7 8 9 10
11 12 13 14 15 16

2 CORINTHIANS
1 2 3 4 5 6 7 8 9 10
11 12 13

GALATIANS
1 2 3 4 5 6

EPHESIANS
1 2 3 4 5 6

PHILIPPIANS
1 2 3 4

COLOSSIANS
1 2 3 4

1 THESSALONIANS
1 2 3 4 5

2 THESSALONIANS
1 2 3

1 TIMOTHY
1 2 3 4 5 6

2 TIMOTHY
1 2 3 4

NEW TESTAMENT

TITUS
1 2 3

PHILEMON
1

HEBREWS
1 2 3 4 5 6 7 8 9 10
11 12 13

JAMES
1 2 3 4 5

1 PETER
1 2 3 4 5

2 PETER
1 2 3

1 JOHN
1 2 3 4 5

2 JOHN
1

3 JOHN
1

JUDE
1

REVELATION
1 2 3 4 5 6 7 8 9 10
11 12 13 14 15 16 17 18 19 20
21 22

Book of the Bible STUDY

BOOK _____

CHAPTER _____

WHO IS THE AUTHOR OF THIS BOOK?

WHO WAS THIS BOOK WRITTEN FOR?

WHAT IS THE SETTING?

WORD	DEFINITION	SYNONYMS

MAIN POINTS (SUMMARY)

GOD'S PROMISES / ATTRIBUTES / ACTIONS

Book of the Bible STUDY

BOOK _____

CHAPTER _____

RELATED SCRIPTURES

MY THOUGHTS (QUESTIONS & APPLICATIONS

COMPARISONS FROM ANOTHER TRANSLATION

Character Study

BOOK _____

CHAPTER _____

NAME

WHERE HE / SHE LIVED

APPROXIMATE DATE HE / SHE LIVED

FAMILY / RELATED TO

KNOWN FOR

POSITIVE CHARACTER TRAITS

NEGATIVE CHARACTER TRAITS

BIGGEST OBTACLES

BIGGEST VICTORIES

WHAT ROLE DID THIS PERSON PLAY IN GOD'S PLAN

You should be known for the beauty THAT COMES FROM WITHIN, the *unfading beauty* of a gentle and quiet spirit, WHICH IS SO PRECIOUS to God.

1 Peter 3:4

Grace Bible Study Method

BOOK _____

CHAPTER _____

G — **GREET** God and invite Him to be part of your quiet time.

R — **READ** the passage at least twice.

A — **ANALYZE** and apply.
- What happened in this passage?
- What did you learn through this text?
- How can I apply this passage to my life?

C — **CHARACTER** and attributes of God.
  What did you learn about God's character and attributes through this passage?

E — **EXALT** and praise God for His flawless character, spend time in prayers.

Bible Study for Women: *Made Amazingly Simple*

Grace Bible Study Method

BOOK _____

CHAPTER _____

G
GREET God and invite Him to be part of your quiet time.

_____
_____
_____

R
READ the passage at least twice.

_____
_____
_____

A
ANALYZE and apply.

_____
_____
_____

C
CHARACTER and attributes of God.

_____
_____
_____

E
EXALT and praise God for His flawless character, spend time in prayers.

_____
_____
_____

Read Bible
STUDY METHOD

BOOK _____

CHAPTER _____

R

READ and reflect on the passage.
- Read the passage at least two times.
- Note where the text takes place.
- Note who the author is and who the text is written to.

E

EVALUATE the passage.
- Summarize the text.
- What are the repeated words in the text?
- What are the keywords in the passage?
- What is the overall theme of this passage?
- What questions do you have after reading this?

A

APPLY the passage to your life.
- What did I learn through this passage?
- What action is God calling me to take?
- How can I live this text in action?
- Who is God calling me to pray for or minister to after reading this passage?

D

DELIGHT in God's presence.
- Praise God for who He is and His flawless character.
- Praise the Lord for His sacrifice at the cross.
- Thank God for His many blessings.
- Pray through your prayer requests and ask God to move on behalf of each one.

Read Bible
STUDY METHOD

BOOK _____

CHAPTER _____

R
READ and reflect on the passage.
_____
_____
_____
_____
_____

E
EVALUATE the passage.
_____
_____
_____
_____
_____

A
APPLY the passage to your life.
_____
_____
_____
_____
_____

D
DELIGHT in God's presence.
_____
_____
_____
_____
_____

TOPICAL STUDY ON _____

_____ DATE _____

VERSE ON THIS TOPIC

VERSE ON THIS TOPIC

VERSE ON THIS TOPIC

VERSE ON THIS TOPIC

VERSE ON THIS TOPIC

VERSE ON THIS TOPIC

TOPICAL STUDY ON _____

_____ DATE _____

COMMON THEME OF THE VERSES

WHAT DOES HE REQUIRE OF US?

WHAT IS REVEALED ABOUT GOD'S CHARACTER?

WHAT ACTIONS WILL GOD DO?

SUMMARY OF VERSES

APPLICATION

Write the Word

DATE
_____

PASSAGE

CHARACTER OF GOD

ACTIONS OF GOD

GOD'S COMMANDS

GOD'S PROMISES

REPEATED WORDS / PHRASES

APPLICATIONS

Verse Mapping

BOOK _____

CHAPTER /VERSE_____

VERSE / TRANSLATION

MEANING

SYNONYMS

PARALLEL VERSES

APPLICATION

VERSE BEFORE

SIMILARITIES

DIFFERENCES

VERSE BELOW

SIMILARITIES

DIFFERENCES

25 Questions *to Help you Study* God's *Word with* Confidence

WHO

1. Who wrote the passage?
2. Who was it written to?
3. Who are the main characters?
4. Who does God say I am?
5. Who is God calling me to pray after reading the passage?

WHAT

6. What was happening at the culture at the time?
7. What happened in the passage?
8. What did you learn from the passage?
9. What is the overall theme if this passage?
10. What are the keywords on this passage (or words you don't know)?
11. What questions do you have after reading this?
12. What can we learn about God's character?
13. What are God's promises?
14. What actions will God do?
15. What actions am I to take after reading this?

WHEN

16. When did this passage take place?

WHERE

17. Where did this passage take place?
18. Where do you see Jesus or hints of Jesus in this passage?

WHY

19. Why was this passage written?
20. Why is something said or being questioned in this text?
21. Why do you think God allowed or will allow this to happen?

HOW

22. How did these characters and situations speak to me?
23. How does this passage speak to me about my relationship with God?
24. How does this passage speak to me about my relationship with others?
25. How can I apply this to my life?

MEMO

DATE:

MEMO

DATE:

My Anchor Verses

Write a favorite Scripture that points you to
God's promises and renews your mind with truth.

3

PRAY
God's Word

PRAYER
TEMPLATES & ACTIVTIES

PROVERBS 31:29

MANY WOMEN
do *noble* things
but YOU
surpass them
all.

Prayer & Journal Prompts

1 Lord, I praise you for...	**2** God, your character is...	**3** Thank you for your faithfulness...	**4** Thanks for blessing me with...	**5** I surrender my worries to you especially...	**6** Take my fear of ____ Lord...	**7** Help me to trust you with...
8 Give me strength to...	**9** Please forgive me for...	**10** Refine my character in the area of...	**11** Fill my heart with your joy and peace...	**12** Helm me serve my family with love and humility...	**13** I surrender my emotions to you including...	**14** Help me to live free from sin and shame...
15 Give me hope in tough times, especially...	**16** Thank you for your amazing grace at the cross...	**17** Help me to serve others with joy...	**18** Make me generous with my time and resources...	**19** Help me to pause and pray in tough times...	**20** Give me wisdom in all situations including...	**21** Give me strength when I am tempted...
22 Help me boldly share my faith with others...	**23** Help me to love others well in your name...	**24** I pray healing for...	**25** I pray salvation for...	**26** Thank you for loving me even as a sinner...	**27** I praise you for your goodness...	**28** I praise you that your ways are perfect...
29 I praise you for protection and provision...	**30** Thank you for the promise of eternity with you.					

Bible Study for Women: *Made Amazingly Simple*

Prayer Requests

FAMILY

FRIENDS

FINANCES

SELF

MINISTRY

WORLD

PRAISES

Gratitude Journal

Give thanks in all circumstances.

1 Thessalonians 5:18

3 THINGS I AM THANKFUL FOR TODAY

LORD THANK YOU FOR THESE PEOPLE

GOD THANK YOU FOR THESE BLESSINGS

THANK YOU GOD, FOR THESE SITUATIONS THAT STRETCH AND GROW ME

MY REFLECTIONS

MY PRAYER OF THANKS

Monthly Bible Study Planner

| January | February | March | April |

| May | June | July | August |

| September | October | November | December |

Blessed

are the pure in heart: for they shall see God.

Matthew 5:8

Part II

Women of the Bible STUDY

Each section begins with a short background on the woman to give you some context, including *the meaning of her name* which is often a key element of the narrative.

On the character study page, you will find the main scriptures that make up the woman's story.

Take your time to go at your preferred pace through each woman. There is no timeline to give you flexibility. Some, like Leah and Rachel, are recommended to study simultaneously because their stories are interwoven.

She

REACHES OUT TO THE NEEDY; SHE STRETCHES OUT HER HANDS TO THE POOR. DOESN'T FEAR FOR HER HOUSEHOLD WHEN IT SNOWS, BECAUSE THEY ARE ALL DRESSED IN WARM CLOTHES.

Proverbs 31:20-21

Eve
POWERFUL PURPOSE

> The Lord God said, "It is not good for the man to be alone. I will make a *helper* suitable for him."
>
> Genesis 2:18

MEANING OF HER NAME

Her name is **c̲hava** in Hebrew, which has a root connection with the verb **l̲ichyot** *"to live"*, and words such as **chai** and **c̲hayim** communicating the idea of *"life"*.

BACKGROUND INFORMATION

Eve is described as **"helper"** in Genesis 2:18. The word in Hebrew for helper is "ezer". This word is a combination of two roots, one meaning "to rescue," "to save," and the other meaning "to be strong."

This word "ezer" is used throughout the Scriptures to describe how God will come to the rescue and help of his people. Eve is created as a powerful help, that offers something to her partnerships that is strong and needed. We begin to see how God is purposely distinguishing women from all the other animals. She will be—unlike the animals—a power (or strength) equal to him. This idea is further reinforced when God creates Eve from Adam's side. It's creating an image of a powerful side-by-side relationship, designed to fulfill God's purposes to be "*fruitful and increase in number; fill the earth and subdue it. Rule over the fish in the sea and the birds in the sky and over every living creature that moves on the ground*" (Genesis 1:28) While Eve may be known for her mistakes, her story has more to unfold as we get to the heart of a woman, mother, and her God given purpose.

Bible Study for Women: Made Amazingly Simple | 65

Character Study

Eve

KEY SCRIPTURES
- ☐ Genesis 1:24-31
- ☐ Genesis 2:15-25
- ☐ Genesis 3:1-4:1
- ☐ Genesis 4:25

BIBLICAL TRUTHS ILLUSTRATED IN HER LIFE

STRENGTHS

WEAKNESSES

KEY LIFE EVENTS AND DETAILS

PERSONAL OBSERVATIONS

DATE   /   /

REFLECTION

WHAT DOES THIS TEACH ME ABOUT GOD?

WHAT DOES THIS TEACH ME ABOUT MANKIND?

PERSONAL REFLECTION

WHAT IS GOD TEACHING ME?

HOW CAN I APPLY THIS TO MY LIFE?

PRAYER

Journal

Sarah
DAUGHTER OF THE KING

> Sarah said, "God has brought me laughter, and everyone who hears about this will laugh with me."
>
> Genesis 21:6

MEANING OF HER NAME

God changed Sarai's name, meaning *"my princess"* to Sarah, meaning *"mother of nations"* or *"princess of many"* (Gen. 17:15)

BACKGROUND INFORMATION

Sarah and her husband Abraham would have lived a nomadic life, as her husband followed God's invitation to leave home and go to the land He would reveal. This patriarchal era is important to us. Through Abraham and his descendants, God began to develop a people of His own. The Abrahamic Covenant *(God's unconditional pledge to Abraham)* contains many precious promises: Abraham would have numerous offspring; his descendants would possess the land of Canaan, and God would bless all people through this nation.

As we will see, Sarah plays a crucial role in partnering with God to bring about his promises. Even her name change speaks of this. She will be the *"mother of nations."* Sarah will wrestle with her faith, and believing God's promises. She will be the most mentioned woman in the scriptures.

However, as we dive into the New Testament, her legacy is truly fitting of a **Royal Princess in God's kingdom.**

Bible Study for Women: *Made Amazingly Simple* | 69

Character STUDY

Sarah

KEY SCRIPTURES
- [ ] Genesis 12
- [ ] Genesis 16
- [ ] Genesis 17:1-22
- [ ] Genesis 21:1-20
- [ ] Hebrews 11:11
- [ ] Galatians 4:21-31
- [ ] 1 Peter 3:5-6

BIBLICAL TRUTHS ILLUSTRATED IN HER LIFE

STRENGTHS

WEAKNESSES

KEY LIFE EVENTS AND DETAILS

PERSONAL OBSERVATIONS

DATE   /   /

REFLECTION

WHAT DOES THIS TEACH ME ABOUT GOD?

WHAT DOES THIS TEACH ME ABOUT MANKIND?

PERSONAL REFLECTION

WHAT IS GOD TEACHING ME?

HOW CAN I APPLY THIS TO MY LIFE?

PRAYER

Journal

Rebekah
SURRENDERED STRENGTH

> Isaac prayed to the Lord on behalf of his wife, because she was childless. The Lord answered his prayer, and his wife Rebekah became pregnant.
>
> Genesis 25:21

MEANING OF HER NAME

Rebekah in Hebrew is **riv'qah** which means *"Tied Up, Secured"*.

BACKGROUND INFORMATION

Rebekah in the Bible was the wife of Isaac and mother of Jacob and Esau. We first meet Rebekah in Genesis 24:15, where she is identified as *"the daughter of Bethuel son of Milkah, who was the wife of Abraham's brother Nahor."* This would have made Rebekah a great-niece to Abraham and Sarah. Isaac. Abraham had been looking for a wife for his son Isaac, but did not want him to marry a Canaanite. Rebekah's story begins with Abraham's servant coming to her town, praying to find the right woman for Isaac.

Rebekah's marriage to Isaac was the result of God's providence. Her pregnancy was an answer to prayer, and the lives of her sons fulfilled prophecy. We see in Rebekah a mix of faithful living, and personal striving to get her way. Her family will be filled with favorites, rivalry, lies and deceit. We begin to see how despite our sin God through his mercy and wisdom, can ultimately bring about his will. Will we live in surrender to God's will and timing, or will we forcefully make our own desires come about in our family? Rebekah's story invites us into God's divine story, and to reflect on our role in partnering with God to bring about his plans for our family.

Character STUDY

Rebekah

KEY SCRIPTURES
- [ ] Genesis 24
- [ ] Genesis 25:19-34
- [ ] Genesis 26:34-28:9
- [ ] Romans 9:8-16

BIBLICAL TRUTHS ILLUSTRATED IN HER LIFE

STRENGTHS

WEAKNESSES

KEY LIFE EVENTS AND DETAILS

PERSONAL OBSERVATIONS

DATE   /   /

REFLECTION

WHAT DOES THIS TEACH ME
ABOUT GOD?

WHAT DOES THIS TEACH ME
ABOUT MANKIND?

PERSONAL REFLECTION

WHAT IS GOD TEACHING ME?

HOW CAN I APPLY THIS TO MY LIFE?

PRAYER

Journal

Leah

GOD'S KINDNESS IN A MEAN WORLD

MEANING OF HER NAME

Her name is **ay-aw** in Hebrew, which means **"weary"**.

BACKGROUND INFORMATION

Leah's father Laban, believed the only way to get his daughter married was to trick someone into marrying her. So that is what he did. He tricked Jacob into marrying Leah, even though Jacob was in love with her beautiful sister, Rachel. But the Lord had compassion on Leah and allowed her to flourish as a mother (Genesis 29:31). Leah bore a son, whom she named Reuben. His name sounds similar to the Hebrew word that means **"he has seen my misery."** As Leah had more kids, Rachel became jealous because she was barren.

Leah was treated poorly by her husband and sister, but God blessed her richly in the form of motherhood. Her third son, Levi, became the father of the tribe of Israel that was chosen to serve the Lord as priests in the tabernacle and later the temple. Her fourth son, Judah, became the father of the line through which God carried out His covenant with Jacob's grandfather Abraham. God had promised that one day all people would be blessed through Abraham's seed (Genesis 12:1–3; 22:17–18). Later, he revealed that this Messiah would come from the tribe of Judah. Jesus was of the tribe of Judah and therefore a descendant of Leah. Despite the love others withheld from Leah, her story invites us to discover God's goodness and lovingkindness woven into the fabric of the hard days of life.

> When the LORD saw that Leah was not loved, he enabled her to conceive
>
> Genesis 29:31

Character STUDY

Leah

KEY SCRIPTURES
- ☐ Genesis 29
- ☐ Genesis 30
- ☐ Genesis 31
- ☐ Ruth 4:11

BIBLICAL TRUTHS ILLUSTRATED IN HER LIFE

STRENGTHS

WEAKNESSES

KEY LIFE EVENTS AND DETAILS

PERSONAL OBSERVATIONS

Bible Study for Women: *Made Amazingly Simple* | 78

DATE   /   /

REFLECTION

WHAT DOES THIS TEACH ME
ABOUT GOD?

WHAT DOES THIS TEACH ME
ABOUT MANKIND?

PERSONAL REFLECTION

WHAT IS GOD TEACHING ME?

HOW CAN I APPLY THIS TO MY LIFE?

PRAYER

Journal

Rachel

HOPE IN THE LORD

> When the LORD saw that Leah was not loved, he enabled her to conceive.
>
> Genesis 30:22

MEANING OF HER NAME

Her name is **raw-khale'** in Hebrew, which means *"ewe"* or *"female sheep"*.

BACKGROUND INFORMATION

Rachel is the daughter of Laban, younger sister to Leah, and the favorite wife of Jacob. Jacob is fleeing Esau when he comes to his Uncle Laban's home, and quickly falls in love with the beautiful Rachel. He agrees to work 7 years to marry her, but says *"they seemed like only a few days to him because of his love."* Laban then, tricks Jacob into marrying Leah first, and Jacob agrees to work another 7 years to marry his love, Rachel.

While Jacob's love for Rachel is passionate, her inability to have kids consumes her. Her jealousy of her sister Leah runs deep. Rachel, follows the custom of the time and gives her servant Bilhah to Jacob to bear children for her. One day, Rachel so desperately wanted Leah's mandrakes, believing that this root would help make her fertile, so she traded a night with Jacob for the mandrakes. Her sister Leah become pregnant that night.

The desire for motherhood runs so deep for many women, and for Rachel this felt like her entire life's purpose. She was loved, yet unfulfilled. Where will God meet her in this struggle? How will God refine her character through the trials? Her story unfolds through beauty, tears, and longing.

Character STUDY

Rachel

KEY SCRIPTURES
- ☐ Genesis 29
- ☐ Genesis 30
- ☐ Genesis 31
- ☐ Ruth 4:11

BIBLICAL TRUTHS ILLUSTRATED IN HER LIFE

STRENGTHS

WEAKNESSES

KEY LIFE EVENTS AND DETAILS

PERSONAL OBSERVATIONS

Bible Study for Women: *Made Amazingly Simple* | 82

DATE   /   /

REFLECTION

WHAT DOES THIS TEACH ME ABOUT GOD?

WHAT DOES THIS TEACH ME ABOUT MANKIND?

PERSONAL REFLECTION

WHAT IS GOD TEACHING ME?

HOW CAN I APPLY THIS TO MY LIFE?

PRAYER

Journal

Jochebed
COURAGEOUS HOPE

> By faith Moses' parents hid him for three months after he was born, because they saw he was no ordinary child, and they were not afraid of the king's edict.
>
> Hebrews 11:23

MEANING OF HER NAME

Her name is a combination of **Yah** and **kabed**. "Yah" is commonly accepted as a shortened form of **Yahweh**. "Kabed" means heavy, or impressive, and is often translation **"Glory"**. Jochebed means ***"Yahweh is Glory"***.

BACKGROUND INFORMATION

Jochebed is the wife of Amram and mother of Moses, Aaron and Miriam (Exodus 6:20, Numbers 26:59). The narrative in Exodus 2 about Moses' birth introduces her, but without providing her name. We simply know she is a from the priestly tribe Levi and marries a Levitical man.

Her story picks up more than 200 years after the death of Joseph (Gen 50:26) and the Hebrews are now under a new Pharaoh who is suspicious of their large population. He is afraid that they may turn against him and leave Egypt. So, he ruthlessly enslaves them, oppresses them and makes their lives bitter. Finally, he orders the Hebrew midwives to kill all the boys that are born. In a twist of irony, it is the women, like Jochebed, who rise to defy Pharoah and fight for lives of their children. They fear God above Pharaoh and do not kill the male infants. Pharaoh then commands all his people to throw the babies into the Nile river. No male baby is safe now. The story of Jochebed, the mother of Moses, begins here in unbearable circumstances. She invites us to trust along with her, in our God who is greater than all circumstances and has with a heart to rescue and save his people.

Character Study

Jochebed

KEY SCRIPTURES
- Exodus 1:11-22
- Exodus 2:1-11
- Hebrews 11:23
- Exodus 14:10-31

BIBLICAL TRUTHS ILLUSTRATED IN HER LIFE

STRENGTHS

WEAKNESSES

KEY LIFE EVENTS AND DETAILS

PERSONAL OBSERVATIONS

DATE   /   /

REFLECTION

WHAT DOES THIS TEACH ME
ABOUT GOD?

WHAT DOES THIS TEACH ME
ABOUT MANKIND?

PERSONAL REFLECTION

WHAT IS GOD TEACHING ME?

HOW CAN I APPLY THIS TO MY LIFE?

PRAYER

Journal

Hannah

A PRAYING WOMAN

> There is no one holy like the Lord; there is no one besides you; there is no Rock like our God.
>
> 1 Samuel 2:2

MEANING OF HER NAME

Her name is **Channâh** in Hebrew, which means *"grace"* or *"favored"*.

BACKGROUND INFORMATION

Hannah's story takes place in the Judges era of the Bible. The Israelites are living in the promised land ruled by judges under the guidance of prophets. Hannah is married, and very much loved by her husband, Elkanah. However, Hannah was very grieved. She desperately desired a child, but could not conceive. To make matters worse, Peninnah, Elkanah's other wife, taunted Hannah concerning her barrenness. Her unkindness on top of her own grief, was too much for her to bear. Hannah cries out to God, making promises to Him if he would give her son.

She visits the temple in Jerusalem, a long journey from her home in the hill country of Ephraim. While Hannah was pouring her heart out to God, Eli (the priest at the tabernacle) saw her and mistook her distress for drunkenness. We see her faith as she leaves the temple. God has not yet answered her prayers, but she leaves with a peaceful soul. She rejoices in God's ability to make a weakling strong!

Hannah's story gives us insight into God's heart. God does not despise human desire. Hannah's longing for a child was obviously placed in her heart by God Himself. As we too wrestle with unmet godly desires, her story beckons us to resist the urge to dismiss our desires, but rather continually bring them before our God in prayer!

Character STUDY

KEY SCRIPTURES

- [ ] 1 Samuel 1
- [ ] 1 Samuel 2:1-26
- [ ] 1 Samuel 3 (story of her son)

BIBLICAL TRUTHS ILLUSTRATED IN HER LIFE

STRENGTHS

WEAKNESSES

KEY LIFE EVENTS AND DETAILS

PERSONAL OBSERVATIONS

DATE   /   /

REFLECTION

WHAT DOES THIS TEACH ME ABOUT GOD?

WHAT DOES THIS TEACH ME ABOUT MANKIND?

PERSONAL REFLECTION

WHAT IS GOD TEACHING ME?

HOW CAN I APPLY THIS TO MY LIFE?

PRAYER

Journal

Widow of Zarephath
DEATH AND RESURRECTION

> She opens her arms to the poor and extends her hands to the needy.
>
> Proverbs 31:20

MEANING OF HER NAME

We do not ever get to know her name. However, it's interesting to note that Zarephath means **"refinery."** Zarephath was known for one thing: it was the place where the idols for the worship of Baal were manufactured.

BACKGROUND INFORMATION

There has been a drought in the land of Israel for years. The widow of Zarephath is in dire circumstances. She has lost her husband who would have helped care for and financially support the family. The drought has caused a food shortage, and she is on her last handful of grain to feed her and her son. This is when Elijah shows up asking her for some food and water. Elijah came to Zarephath to this specific widow because God asked him to. God is powerfully at work in both their lives.

The generosity, hospitality and faith of the widow bring about miraculous encounters as all three depend on God to provide. Through so much loss and suffering, we see the light of goodness cast out the darkest nights and trials. The unlikely people who God may use to restore our family, and invigorate our spirits are the heartbeat of this woman's story. As a single, struggling mom with a son to care for, she is a beautiful picture of a woman of valor. As we survey our own lives, will we embrace the city of **"refining"** God may bring us into, so that we may see God's glory breathe new life into existence.

Character Study

Widow of Zarephath

KEY SCRIPTURES
☐ 1 Kings 17

BIBLICAL TRUTHS ILLUSTRATED IN HER LIFE

STRENGTHS

WEAKNESSES

KEY LIFE EVENTS AND DETAILS

PERSONAL OBSERVATIONS

DATE   /   /

REFLECTION

WHAT DOES THIS TEACH ME ABOUT GOD?

WHAT DOES THIS TEACH ME ABOUT MANKIND?

PERSONAL REFLECTION

WHAT IS GOD TEACHING ME?

HOW CAN I APPLY THIS TO MY LIFE?

PRAYER

Journal

Naomi

GOD WHO RESTORES

> Then the women said to Naomi, *"Blessed be the LORD, who has not left you this day without a redeemer, and may his name be renowned in Israel!"*
>
> Ruth 4:14

MEANING OF HER NAME

Her name is **Noʻŏmîy** in Hebrew, which means *"my delight"* or *"pleasant"*.

Later, she will choose to change her name to **Mara**, which means *"bitter"*.

BACKGROUND INFORMATION

When a famine hits Judea, Elimelech and Naomi and their two boys relocate to Moab. There, Mahlon and Kilion marry two Moabite women, Orpah and Ruth. After about tenyears, tragedy strikes. Elimelech dies, and both of Naomi's sons also die, leaving Naomi, Ruth, and Orpah widows. Naomi hears the famine is over and intends to return. In care for her daughters-in-law, she urges them to return to their families, remarry and start afresh. In a sad, heartfelt goodbye, Orpah does just this. However, Ruth chooses to go with Naomi.

The book of Ruth is a story about God, and how he restores those who look to him with hope. It shows how God works in mundane, everyday events in the lives of his people. Naomi loses her entire family early in this story. But these tragedies do not surprise God, and he's able to steer Naomi's losses back into restoration. Naomi's dark night of the soul becomes part of the story of God bringing King David to Israel. God is already weaving her story of redemption. The Book of Ruth invites us to view our day-to-day lives as part of God's bigger plan for our lives and world. Will we see the mundane with expectant hope for God's plan to unfold?

Character STUDY

KEY SCRIPTURES
- [ ] Ruth 1
- [ ] Ruth 2
- [ ] Ruth 3
- [ ] Ruth 4

BIBLICAL TRUTHS ILLUSTRATED IN HER LIFE

STRENGTHS

WEAKNESSES

KEY LIFE EVENTS AND DETAILS

PERSONAL OBSERVATIONS

DATE   /   /

REFLECTION

WHAT DOES THIS TEACH ME
ABOUT GOD?

WHAT DOES THIS TEACH ME
ABOUT MANKIND?

PERSONAL REFLECTION

WHAT IS GOD TEACHING ME?

HOW CAN I APPLY THIS TO MY LIFE?

PRAYER

Journal

Ruth

LOYALTY AND INTEGRITY

> Where you go I will go, and where you stay I will stay. Your people will be my people and your God my God.
>
> Ruth 1:16

MEANING OF HER NAME

Her name is **rut** and means *"friendship"*.

BACKGROUND INFORMATION

Ruth is from Moab, and marries an Israelite when his family comes to Moab due to a famine. Soon after, Ruth's husband dies, along with the other men of the family. Ruth must now choose: follow her mother-in-law. Naomi, back to Israel or return to her family?

Moabites have a long enemy history with Israel, and Ruth knows she would be an outsider. Yet, she breaks social conventions to do right by Naomi. Ruth trusts in Yahweh and commits herself to his people!

Later, Ruth meets and makes the offer of marriage to Boaz in an upstanding way, which is culturally honorable at the time, not scandalous. God honors Ruth's integrity and diligence by weaving her into the big story of salvation. Boaz is a no-nonsense man of character, principle, and responsibility. Boaz is offered as a model of obedience to the Torah in his treatment of the poor. God uses his integrity to save a widow's family and he becomes the ancestor of the Messiah. It's all woven together in God's hands.

This story shows how God is constructing his grand story out of the small, seemingly inconsequential stories of everyday people. It begs us to see our lives also, as being woven into God's grand story.

Character Study

Ruth

KEY SCRIPTURES
- ☐ Ruth 1
- ☐ Ruth 2
- ☐ Ruth 3
- ☐ Ruth 4

BIBLICAL TRUTHS ILLUSTRATED IN HER LIFE

STRENGTHS

WEAKNESSES

KEY LIFE EVENTS AND DETAILS

PERSONAL OBSERVATIONS

DATE   /   /

REFLECTION

WHAT DOES THIS TEACH ME ABOUT GOD?

WHAT DOES THIS TEACH ME ABOUT MANKIND?

PERSONAL REFLECTION

WHAT IS GOD TEACHING ME?

HOW CAN I APPLY THIS TO MY LIFE?

PRAYER

Journal

Elizabeth
REJOICE IN THE LORD

MEANING OF HER NAME

Her name in Greek is **'ĕlĭšeḇaʿ**' but comes from Hebrew origin, **elisabet** meaning *"God is an oath"*.

BACKGROUND INFORMATION

In the opening chapter of Luke, not one, but two women of faith experience miraculous pregnancies. We meet Elizabeth first. She is the wife of Zechariah, a priest, and we are told *"both of them were righteous before God, living blamelessly according to all the commandments and regulations of the Lord"* (1:6). Yet, they had been unable to have a child until the Lord intervened. Soon though, she would give birth to John, who became famously known as John the Baptist.

Around the same time, unbeknownst to Elizabeth, her young relative Mary has also become pregnant through the Lord's intervention. Presumably Mary lived near Nazareth, and Elizabeth lived near Jerusalem where her husband worked in the temple. The shared experience of these two women quickly draws them together. Elizabeth instantly and prophetically knows what has happened to Mary. Elizabeth blesses Mary with the same blessing Deborah, the judge and prophet, once pronounced on the brave and bold Jael. They celebrate and encourage each other in what God's unfolding in their lives.

Their stories invite us to ask how we might be a source of help and support to one another. We can encourage boldness and inspire faith as we identify God's work in in our lives and the lives of others. May our hearts also leap for joy at God's work!

> Blessed is she who has believed that the Lord would fulfill his promises to her!
>
> Luke 1:45

Bible Study for Women: Made Amazingly Simple

Character Study

Elizabeth

KEY SCRIPTURES
- ☐ Luke 1:1-25
- ☐ Luke 1:26-56
- ☐ Luke 1:57-80

BIBLICAL TRUTHS ILLUSTRATED IN HER LIFE

STRENGTHS

WEAKNESSES

KEY LIFE EVENTS AND DETAILS

PERSONAL OBSERVATIONS

DATE   /   /

REFLECTION

WHAT DOES THIS TEACH ME
ABOUT GOD?

WHAT DOES THIS TEACH ME
ABOUT MANKIND?

PERSONAL REFLECTION

WHAT IS GOD TEACHING ME?

HOW CAN I APPLY THIS TO MY LIFE?

PRAYER

Journal

Mary
A MOTHER'S INFLUENCE

My soul magnifies the Lord and my spirit rejoices in God my Savior

Luke 1:46

MEANING OF HER NAME

Her name in Greek is **maria** but comes from Hebrew origin, **miryām**. The meaning is not known for certain, but there are several theories including "rebelliousness". However it was most likely originally an Egyptian name, perhaps derived in part from my *"beloved"* or my *"love"*.

BACKGROUND INFORMATION

Many are familiar with Mary's story. She was betrothed in marriage to Joseph, when an angel appeared to announce she will miraculously become pregnant and give birth to the awaited Messiah. She found favor with God, and embraces the role with faith and joy.

I encourage you to study her mothering side-by-side with Elizabeth. Two women, full of faith and excitement of what God is doing. After all, God had been silent for 400 years until Zechariah received news his wife Elizabeth would conceive. No doubt, these two women share an experience, and birth a story to change history. The Lord is at work in each of their lives, and they name it out loud for each other, like joyous sparks flying between them.

Often, God is moving in ways we don't expect, but we are continually invited into His mysterious ways to bring His kingdom to earth. Mothers partnering with God, have a powerful influence into nurturing and celebrating the works of God!

Character Study

KEY SCRIPTURES
- ☐ Luke 1:26-56
- ☐ Luke 2:1-52
- ☐ John 2:1-12
- ☐ John 19:25-30
- ☐ Acts 1:14

BIBLICAL TRUTHS ILLUSTRATED IN HER LIFE

STRENGTHS

WEAKNESSES

KEY LIFE EVENTS AND DETAILS

PERSONAL OBSERVATIONS

DATE   /   /

REFLECTION

WHAT DOES THIS TEACH ME
ABOUT GOD?

WHAT DOES THIS TEACH ME
ABOUT MANKIND?

PERSONAL REFLECTION

WHAT IS GOD TEACHING ME?

HOW CAN I APPLY THIS TO MY LIFE?

PRAYER

Journal

Lydia
NURTURING A WELCOMING HOME

> After Paul and Silas came out of the prison, they went to Lydia's house, where they met with the brothers and sisters and encouraged them.
>
> Acts 16:40

MEANING OF HER NAME

Her name is **Λυδία** in Greek, which means one who comes from the region in Asia minor called **Lydia**. Some say it could also mean *"beautiful one"* or *"noble one"* in Greek.

BACKGROUND INFORMATION

Lydia came from Thyatira, a city in the western province of Lydia in Asia Minor. Although a gentile, she worshipped God and observed the Sabbath. God strategically reroutes Paul's journey to Philippi, a leading city of Macedonia. Here, he meets Lydia, a wealthy and influential businesswoman, who sold articles dyed purple, a prized color made from certain mollusks. She had a spacious home that could accommodate many guests and servants to meet their needs. This had to be a rare achievement in her day. She surely must have been a hardworking, bold, intelligent woman to achieve the success she enjoyed. She hears the good news from Paul, and enthusiastically devotes her life to Jesus.

We can assume she is a mother since members of her household were baptized. Her home, like many of our homes, becomes a place of sanctuary and rest for the other believers. Her love for Jesus inspired her to use her resources to bless the church family. Smart, strong, and influential, we dive into Lydia's divine story. Here we can begin to dream with God about how our businesses, endeavors, resources, and homes can become avenues of His great love!

Bible Study for Women: *Made Amazingly Simple* | 113

Character STUDY

Lydia

KEY SCRIPTURES
- [ ] Acts 16

BIBLICAL TRUTHS ILLUSTRATED IN HER LIFE

STRENGTHS

WEAKNESSES

KEY LIFE EVENTS AND DETAILS

PERSONAL OBSERVATIONS

DATE   /   /

REFLECTION

WHAT DOES THIS TEACH ME ABOUT GOD?

WHAT DOES THIS TEACH ME ABOUT MANKIND?

PERSONAL REFLECTION

WHAT IS GOD TEACHING ME?

HOW CAN I APPLY THIS TO MY LIFE?

PRAYER

Journal

LIST *of* Positive & Negative *Character Qualities*

> The List on the next two pages will be useful in identifying strengths and weakness. It is not exhaustive, but a place to start.

LIST of Positive Traits

- Honesty
- Integrity
- Dependability
- Loyalty
- Dedication
- Faithfulness
- Trustworthiness
- Sincerity
- Diligence
- Orderliness
- Righteousness
- Fairness
- Obedience
- Courteousness
- Respectfulness
- Reverence
- Deference
- Gratefulness
- Thankfulness
- Wisdom
- Discernment
- Sensitivity
- Perspective
- Discreetness
- Carefulness
- Cautiousness
- Discipline
- Thriftiness
- Good Stewardship
- Resourcefulness
- Observer
- Industry
- Creativity
- Enthusiasm
- Cheerfulness
- Lovingness
- Kindness
- Patience
- Self-Denying
- Self-Giving
- Sacrificing
- Compassionate
- Humbleness
- Sympathy
- Generosity
- Forgiveness
- Gentleness
- Mercifulness
- Peacemaking
- Self-Control
- Perseverance
- Stableness
- Balance
- Cleanliness
- Confidence
- Boldness
- Courageousness
- Calmness
- Flexibleness
- Sense of Humor

LIST of NEGATIVE Traits

- Unfaithful
- Unreliable
- Slanderer
- Gossiper
- Compromising
- Flatterer
- Lazy
- Shallow
- Hypocritical
- Crafty/Sly
- Deceitful
- Dishonest
- Unfair
- Insulting
- Rebellious
- Tyrannical
- Disobedient
- Ungrateful
- Shortsighted
- Halfhearted
- Foolish
- Talkative
- Idolatrous
- Careless
- Forgetful
- Wasteful
- Cruel
- Selfish
- Insensitive
- Prejudiced
- Unforgiving
- Harsh
- Grudging
- Indifferent
- Apathetic
- Cowardly
- Impulsive
- Proud
- Wavering
- Stubborn
- Sensual
- Greedy
- Fearful
- Jealous
- Bitter
- Complaining
- Disrespectful
- Manipulative
- Worldly
- A Worrier
- Self-Righteous
- Fears man
- A doubter
- Violent
- Gluttonous
- Immoral
- Vain
- Lusts for Power
- Controlling
- Forgets God

Want more ways to *Connect to God through* Scripture?

WE'VE GOT OTHER PRODUCTS TO GO WITH STUDY AND MUCH MUCH MORE!

Visit amazingwords.com

Made in the USA
Coppell, TX
01 July 2024

34159392R00072